Movin' On!
A Kid's Guide To Skagway, Alaska

Photography by John D. Weigand
Poetry by Penelope Dyan

Bellissima Publishing, LLC
Jamul, California
www.bellissimapublishing.com

Copyright © 2013 by Penny D. Weigand and John D. Weigand

All rights reserved. No part of this book may be reproduced or transmitted in any form or by any means, electronic or mechanical, including photocopying, recording, or by any other means, or by any information or storage retrieval system, without permission from the publisher.

ISBN 978-1-61477-106-7
First Edition

The quest for treasure includes more than mere silver and gold.

PENELOPE DYAN

Movin' On!
Bellissima Publishing, LLC

Introduction

Skagway, Alaska celebrates its gold rush past; and if you go there you can ride a train high into the mountains and on a clear day see all the way to the sea. There is a quaint, preserved town that you can walk through to your heart's content where you can shop, snack, walk, ride in a horse and buggy and just enjoy the quiet simplicity of this town that bills itself as the gateway of the Klondike Gold Rush of 1898! And when you see the breadth of the land and the cold mountains covered in snow, you can visualize the hardship these prospectors went through in their search for the golden ore.

Written by award winning author, attorney and former teacher, Penelope Dyan, to accompany photographs taken by the talented photographer, John D. Weigand, you can take a peek at this place right out of the past as you practice your reading skills through the use of word recognition, word repetition and rhyme. And if you happen to take a trip to Alaska, this book is the perfect size for little hands to hold and stuff with all their tickets and other things! There is also a music video on the Bellissimavideo YouTube Channel with the same name as this book, with even more pictures of this grand place, to add to your learning fun. So go over bridges and go through tunnels and say hello to a bunch of rocks using this book and your imagination!

Movin' On!
Bellissima Publishing, LLC

Movin' On!
A Kid's Guide To Skagway, Alaska

Photography by John D. Weigand
Poetry by Penelope Dyan

In Beautiful Skagway, Alaska,
you can see the green of the trees.
You can see snow kissed mountains.
And you can feel the cool breeze.

In town, if you are in luck,
you might find a dog
ready to drive a truck.

And this, they will tell you,
is the little engine that could.
It used to run up and down
the mountain
fueled by wood.

In Skagway you can take a train,
up through tunnels and mountains,
right through the wild terrain,
where once prospectors
searched for gold,
through sleet and snow
and blizzards cold.

You will wind up the mountains,
and you can't wait,
as you follow the path of
the Klondike Gold Rush of of 1898!

Your train travels below a ridge,
into a tunnel across a narrow bridge.

Your train goes clickety clack,
along the rails,
as the train conductor points
out those old prospector trails.
You reach the snow filled mountains
at the very top,
and then the train comes to a stop.
Then back down the tracks
and into town you go,
leaving behind you the mountains
and the snow!

And you see everything all again,
as down the tracks the train travels
around the bend.
Clickety, clickety, clickety clack,
your train goes traveling
back down the track.

And soon after you get down, you decide to walk to the corner of the town.

There are colorful old buildings and plenty to see and do.

Some rocks and a piece of wood, might even say "Hello" to you!

And as the mountains stand
majestically above the glimmering sea,
you decide that today
this is just where you want to be.
Another day will bring adventure new,
and that is quite all right with you.
Your mother tells you it is wise,
to let this beauty fill your eyes.

"Some beauty is in the eyes of the beholder, while other beauty simply is."

Penelope Dyan

www.ingramcontent.com/pod-product-compliance
Ingram Content Group UK Ltd.
Pitfield, Milton Keynes, MK11 3LW, UK
UKHW060134240426
12048UKWH00002B/30